hurt by the sun

hurt by the sun

d. w. alexander

HURT BY THE SUN

ISBN   978-1-63676-369-9 *Paperback*

               978-1-63676-445-0 *Kindle Ebook*

               978-1-63676-370-5 *Ebook*

to those who inspired what follows,

and to those who will inspire what's to come

contents

———

author's note   1

i. sunburnt   3

ii. darkness   59

iii. eclipse   119

iv. sunlight   187

author's note

###

What if our love stories aren't about finding our soul mates, but rather about our journey towards finding ourselves?

People change in relationships. Whether it's in the form of a new hobby, habit, or scar, you often leave a relationship as a slightly different person than the one who entered it.

Most people would probably call this "baggage." I like to think of these bits and pieces as akin to the carving of a statue:

Each relationship chipping away at the marble. Some taking off large chunks. Others unearthing small elegant details. Slowly a figure emerges, with jagged edges and rough skin. Only then is the artist able to tend to the cracks left behind and begin to polish and shine. In doing so, sculpting their vision—or as I would say, finding themselves.

It's not an easy process. Or a straightforward one. But at the end of it all, you're left looking in the mirror at this incredible piece of art—built by not only your experiences and relationships, but also the blood and tears poured into the process of loving yourself.

As I began writing, I saw this theme extend into all aspects of my life. To realize that the risk of being completely open and vulnerable is simply... worth it. From moments of heartbreak and sadness to emotions of pure joy and happiness, these poems dive into the idea that we, as humans, aren't defined by a single moment or event, but instead are a collection of experiences and memories that shape who we are and who we are becoming.

My hope is that, in reading this book, you will feel connected to, or understood by, one the words, phrases, or poems. Each poem is an opportunity to self-reflect about your own story and your own perspective—while also lending the notion that we aren't alone in our shared life experiences. I hope you feel inspired to tear down your own walls, and share and connect with the people in your life; so that you may feel and love fearlessly. So that you may continue to chip away and polish your own sculpture.

I look forward to taking this journey together.

sunburnt

——

Hi..

um..

hello.

I…

meant to say this, before

we shot icicles as arrows
from Cupid's quiver that froze

but..

I was on the moon then, baby

and honestly,

I can't imagine life with—

—*The person you are trying to reach is unavaila—*

it felt good, at first
the way your soft rays kissed my skin
your warmth slowly traveling
across the lines atop my skeleton

but then you began to burn
consuming flesh
until i was nothing
but crumbling dried bone

so here i am,
ashes in a bottle
addicted to your sunburn
hoping that maybe tomorrow
you will rise across the horizon
and find me
once again

it seems perfect now
the morning sun
kissing our cheeks,
but at some point
light will sneak past horizon lines
leaving both of us behind
with nothing
but sheets soaked in memories

incompatible.

a single
crisp leaf
        sways
back
        and forth

f
a
l
l
i
n
g

for
the gravel path

kissing
sharp lips

as
its body
helplessly
breaks in half

leaving behind
a dust
of red memories

i should've told you
that i loved you
one more time

before the melody
left your body
and slowly sputtered away
in the wind

i still hear

the slight quiver in your voice
as teeth speak and rejoice

the nervous laugh
as we describe our future path

the memories we share
as we discuss sea air

the short breath you take
as we both remember

the heartbreak

Simply because I can
does not mean I want to.

—*I do not wish to walk this world*

alone.

there is more to be said in the silence
between our moments of laughter
than in the words leaving our lips

for it is in those gaps of nothing
where truth lies
and lies can no longer sing

what terrible things
your mind shoves down your throat
to keep your heart
from speaking

please swallow words no longer

give me the raw, unfiltered
heartbreaking
truth

just do not give me that same line
of silence

what happened
          that one day
when your eyes turned red
pooling with salty tears

what happened
          that one day
when your face was pressed
against that cold wooden floor

what happened
          that one day
when your blank stare
failed to recognize me

what happened
          that one day
when you surrendered
your freedom

what happened
          that one day
when your love
turned to hate

what happened
          that one day
when trust
turned to anxiety

what happened
       to you

what happened
to make you this way?

in every relationship
there's one moment
that defines your connection

it's the moment held
after love fades
and life cascades

with sand on my back
and sea breeze in your hair
i spoke three words
that left me naked
for the next three years

i'll never forget
that feeling in my chest
when my heart said
"i love you"

the way you
look at me
     terrifies
the way you
touch me
     petrifies
the way you
feel me
     mortifies

I miss
how you smile
when
   other girls
     look at me
I miss
how you kiss
  my scars
    gently
I miss
how you
  crave me

I hate
　the way I look at you
　　because
I hate
　the way I touch you
　　because
I hate
　the way you make me feel
　　because
I love you

and so there she stands.

A fool takes a step forward, confident in his blind leader;
Imprudently trusting of what may lie ahead.
And so there she stands,
Bearing sensual hips and flaxen hair;
Yet where her heart should lie,
Exists an empty crater instead.
The fool was engulfed by its toxicity,
With a burn he cannot shed;
He trusted blindly, and was betrayed and misled.

A brute takes a step forward,
Confident in his senseless vision;
Carelessly trusting of what may lie ahead.
And so there she stands,
Bearing sensual hips and flaxen hair;
Yet where her heart should lie,
Exists an empty crater instead.
The brute believed he could navigate its acidity,
Leaving with his ego fed;
Blinded to his certainty,
He was later found swallowing lead.

An elder takes a step forward,
Confident in his apparent experience;
Assertively trusting of what may lie ahead.
And so there she stands,
Bearing sensual hips and flaxen hair;

Yet where her heart should lie,
Exists an empty crater instead.
The elder fell victim to the purge,
With no one beside his deathbed;
He fatally followed his urge,
His heart ripped out without a word said.

A cripple takes a small step forward,
Confident in his everlasting pain;
Gingerly trusting of what may lie ahead.
And so there she stands,
Bearing sensual hips and flaxen hair;
Yet where her heart should lie,
Exists an empty crater instead.
The cripple had nothing to lose,
A product of what infidelity may take;
Former prey to the superficial blues,
His heart now too cold to break.
When she spoke he realized,
He and she were one in the same;
Her spirit fossilized, product of the everlasting shame.
They were both afraid, fearing the risk of true pain;
The past making love nothing but dismay,
Shadowed with self-blame.
And so there they stand,
Bearing crippling pain and fearing the start;
Yet where their hearts should lie,
Exist two halves that make up one piece of art.

i'm not myself
when i'm with you

i see the words leaving your lips
but hear no sound

i see the creases in your dimples
but hear no smile

all i hear
is my heart
beat

as if nothing else matters

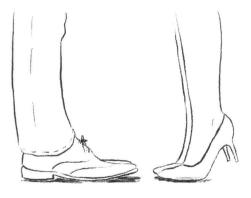

i remember watching you that night

head bobbing, toes tapping
as you reached out to find my gaze
slow sensual sways

pulling me in close
cheek to chest, arms wrapped

bodies beating, smiles singing
as the world faded away

leaving me blinded,
eyes forever unable to stray

stop stopping yourself
i used to say
finally you did one day
and your love began to decay

how can it be
that you taught me
to love
but are unable
to love

me.

we were the flame
that suffocated itself
by burning
a few moments
too quickly

Red Wine.

Gorgeous red hues
Blend with sultry aromas
Head-turning, attention-demanding
A sculptural vision of classic beauty

Opening with enticing scents
Of blue flower and perfumed spice
You whisper of lavender

A tug of opulence
A hint of refined pipe tobacco

Your silky touch overwhelms me
Full-bodied radiance
Elegant acidity

Exploding into velvety complexities
Our chemistry sparks
With teeth staining extracts
That I instantly fall in love with

The finish crescendos into a salty tide
A taste
Still on my tongue
Years later

sleepless nights
tossing
and turning
unable to turn off the lights

images pass through my conscious mind
terrified. i would rather turn blind
my worst fears seared in mind's eye
electrified. i pray they lie

for i cannot live,
if they become reality.
oh everything i'll give,
if they become a fatality.

what are they, you ask?
well, it's quite simple.

i have only loved once
and never want to love again
for that love
is the only love i want
across infinite lifetimes.

still,
you hold a part
of my heart
between the cracks
in your hands

and yet,
i just hope
you find the happiness
you couldn't find
when you held
all of mine

it was the thought of you
that would make my soul dance
and spirit howl
at the sight of the moon

yet now
he does nothing
but whimper
at the sun
in hope for darkness
to fall again

innocence.

a piece of my purity
died that day
pressing fast forward
on my maturity
as my childhood bliss
left me
the same moment
you did

i gave my everything
only to leave with nothing
but fading memories

i loved my hardest
when i had nothing to lose
but you to gain

unknowingly
starting a journey
that would see our hearts
beaten with bruises

leaving me empty
with you
fully fueled

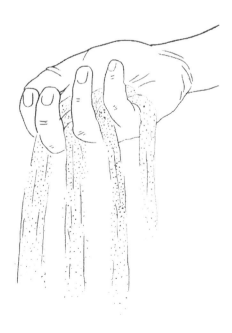

forced to watch
grains of sand
slip through my hourglass hands
helplessly holding
clenched fists
as the final grain drips
and lands

my blistered fingers fumble
in efforts to turn back time
cracking the hourglass figure
that is now a broken shrine

my hands bleed as i struggle
to pick you up again
grain by grain
as my spirit strains
to find the words
    i love you, again

I couldn't let go
even after you
released

me.

Holding onto
the tufts of your sweater
hopelessly
watching you
unravel

me.

my eyes water in attempt to wash away
pictures permanently painted
my throat chokes in attempt to swallow
words once welcomed
my chest burns in attempt to release
soul seared sadness

and still
my heart pumps in hope that one day
you will again fill my lungs with oxygen

It felt warm,
at first;
the kindling you set ablaze.
I was bright and brilliant
vibrating and sparking
from the center of my chest.

But then, came the burning
the smoldering embers
choking lungs
as smoke scorched my throat.

A fire,
too fervid to bear;
engulfing all the air
as it helplessly
found itself
suffocated.

darkness

———

It was twisted. Jaded.
It's sharp edges taunting
The blacksmith as she begins
The soothing. The heating. The healing
In a white hot ember embrace.
Breaking down cool cracked cladding
As tempered marrow becomes molten

Sizzle
Boil
Scream

Let me breathe.
Let me breathe!
Lift me from the embers
Stop the bellows
Release me from this pressure forge

Hammer
Smash

   Let me breathe...

Hammer
Smash

   ...Please?

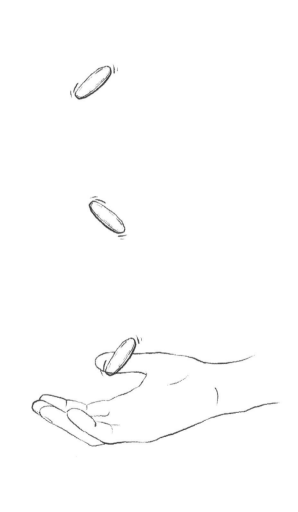

coin flip.

i tossed you with
that same choice today
flip
         flip

twirling
ringing
falling

your imperfect edges
blurring into deceptive
softness
flip
         flip

you finally slip
showing your tail:

caught
in the palm of my hand
i find the same two faces

i do every time you land

i used to pray
to you
hoping your thoughts
would hear my blessings,
my wishful thinking

but now i pray
for you
hoping thoughts
of you
will fade
into distant memories

as i now realize
the angel once loved
became the devil
to which i am chained

blue pill
swallowed

finger tips
locked

body parts
borrowed

souls left
empty

hearts craved

forgetting true
intimacy

comes when
sharing an ordinary moment
becomes special

Why must you go and test the waters?

I see her lips moving
Sighing the words
   I know you are better than them

Them?!

How many must you try
Before your mouth no longer lies
When you tell me
I'm the only one

after the intimacy
how can it be
that i am ready to love
but you so clearly
are not

after the intimacy
how can it be
that i am ready to fight
and have fought
when you have taken the gloves off

after the intimacy
it puzzles me
that you were focused
on cracks between pieces
and not the picture we put together

deciding to knock us off the wall

are you going to tell me what's wrong?

or will you continue
to stain my clean sheets
with your sweaty despair

Conversations.

"You are the one"
—Push

"I have to speak from my heart…"
  —Pull

"I'm not going anywhere"
  —Flip

"Please, don't forget me"
  —Flop

"You define the meaning of true love for me"
  —Well, let's see

"I'll still do anything for you"
  —Please, love me

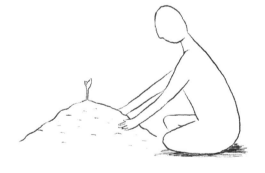

You call this love?
This single sided struggle
to keep you in the clouds
while you kick bits of dirt
into the cracks
between my teeth.

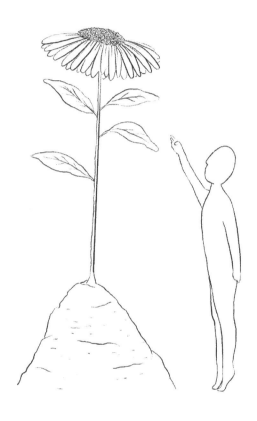

Never enough.
Never enough.
Just more mounds of dirt
as I build you up.

i fell in deep
into your shallow pool
yet still managed to drown
the second time around

the loneliest
i have ever been
was when i fought
for our love

how can
d i s t a n c e
be a part
of healing
when
d i s t a n c e
is the reason
we are
apart?

oh how ironic
    it is
to teach each other
    love
only to end up without
    one another

i admired your insistence
to be exhilarated
to find brightness
among the light

yet it was in that insistence
that you turned away
as you saw how the sun
cast your shadow

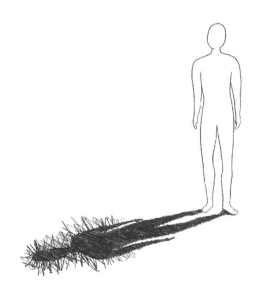

you tossed me aside
like leftover food scraps
after eating my insides
leaving me nothing
but bone

little did you know
it would be those bones
now held inside skin
hard as stones

i did what you asked
reached the summit;
screamed across the mountain tops.
declared my devotion,
tied it to your name.

but it wasn't until
i felt the fibers rip
in my chest
that i knew,
i wouldn't hear an echo.

i can't stop it,
this gifting of me
to you

this grinding of bones
into chalk-white powder
so that you can sprinkle me
atop your elixir;
so that you can
swallow the words
and still say,
love you... too.

It happened again.

My body aches from puppet strings.

One day I'll cut my ties
   —I say
I'll be my own master
   —Just not today

I will pretend to have the situation
under control.
Because I have been taught
to fit your mold.

sometimes i wonder
why you put
the hope in my
hopeless romantics

when in reality
you took away the rom
and left me with
hopeless antics

It was painful.
The way the words left your lips;
the way you described the taste
found between his thighs.

I felt the vomit in my throat,
the bulge of my eye
as you giggled
    Sorry if that was too much

—Sorry?

I swallowed.

—Too much?

I wish I vomited words
to set me free
instead of spitting out
    It's okay

while watching the lies
cling to my face.

Step
     Step
Left
     Right
Left
     Right

Faster. Harder.
Faster. Harder.

Left
     Right
Left
     Right

Muscle fibers scream
Air sacks painfully pop

Still,
You keep going
Showing the whites of your gums
The grit between your teeth
The tears down your cheeks

Until
Finally,
Your chicken feet fail
And you collapse
On cooled pavement

Hoping that maybe,
Maybe this time
You will remain there
In nothing but a pool
Of dead memories

—I, too, have tried to outrun my demons.

i used to love
loving you

but the thought of you
without me…

Scars.

Soft strips of skin
Slight streams of stiches
Soundless screams of sadness

Bloody badges
Brushed blue
Broken blisters

All from you.

Have you ever wept in rain?

It's quite peculiar
to hear teardrops
break in pain.

Unsure where salt
filled sacks begin
and torrent
touches asphalt.

With knee-
        buckling
                tears

Bleeding

As all of it goes
down with drops
of rain.

When I look at him
I see the sadness in his eyes.
Bags bellowing beneath
a tale of long walks
to nowhere
and violent oceans.
Tear.
      Ducts.
            Tapped.

I wonder what creature caused
hazel to be drained
and painted over with a
gray gloomy glaze.

And then I remember—

those eyes are none
other than mine.

eggs.

smash
crack
sizzle

you call from bed
wondering when
i'll be done

flip
sizzle

soon i say
a few more
cracks

rushing
yellow bleeds

soft screams

underutilized
i leave

unfertilized
you grieve

I now measure time
by the parts of me
I've lost.

And darling,
you owe me
a lifetime.

i found myself
suffocated
in the tiny spaces
between your skin
and mine

it's no wonder why
i felt so
deprived
of oxygen

eclipse

———

i never meant for it to happen,
the piercing of skin
as ink pooled
in permanent patterns

and yet
i could never rid my flesh
of imprints left behind
after you carved your name
into my bones

I'll be fine.

You see,
I was born
with rivers
for eyes

but they don't
have the mercy
to fill my lungs
and drown me.

I'm trying
to stitch up the wounds
I cut for you.

It's painful,
pulling together the membrane
to cover up the windows
into my soul.

Stitch
              By
      Stitch

Layer
              By
      Layer

I pinch myself
as your words
slowly fade away.

i was trying to heal
the parts of me
i opened for you

fingers fumble.
wince in pain.
red drops tumble.
pages stain.

i taste irony
trickling down my arms
as this ink seals memories
i didn't want to harm

your fingers fold
                    and
        twist
                    inside me

tossing aside
my organs
in search for my soul

it's a shame;
it was gifted
and now,
i would like it returned

when i asked why
you simply said
everything happens for a reason
little did i know
i was being granted freedom

you were proof
that it's possible
to meet the right person
at the wrong time

i tried to describe you yesterday

i couldn't do it
how could i choose words
to communicate the connection, emotion, and battles
our souls shared
it would be… insufficient

how could anyone understand
the way your love gave port in a storm
the feeling i have when i see your name
the pain i feel when i remember
the tears we shed for each other

how could anyone understand
these soul shackles i bear
to which you hold the keys
as i become nothing
but a ghost keeper

i hate the question.
fully detest.

my tongue quickly spells the word
d i s t a n c e

before my heart can tear
along the stitching
that you placed there;
before i unravel
along the seams
of my bloody repair

still
my heart bursts
in reply,
filling my throat
as i choke

    yes,
    i will
    always
    love you

Sleepless.

Mind racing

Brain beating
Body aching
Heart thinking

Leg tossing
Chest turning

Sleepless nights

Outside honking
Inside screaming

Begging you
To let go

So that I may finally
Rest

Peach Tree.

I frequently dream
Of your peach tree

Reliving the memory
Of sweet treasury

Able to
Pluck plump peaches
Feeling the
Firm fuzzy flesh
Tasting the
Bitter bottom bits

Juices eject
As side effect

Sticky satisfied smile

Yet I awake
Into this nightmare
With branches bare
Dreaming of the orchard
That could've been
Had we both made
Different decisions

I find myself reaching out, grasping
the tufts of their shirts
to pull them in,
thinking their lips will wash away
the pieces of you
still sitting on my tongue.
That their perfume will mask
the smell of you on my sheets.
That their fingerprints will fill
the footprints you left behind.

But maybe I need a spellbinder,
so that I may finally rid
the ghost of you
haunting each of my eyes.

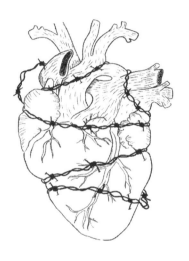

i wonder when
you wrapped your heart
in barbed wire

it never used to sting
when i tried
to love you

but now
i am forced
to walk away,
licking my wounds
like some sort
of animal

i didn't want it to happen, again

this nostalgic cycle
you keep replaying

my heart is fragile, still
and i'm not ready
to have your photograph
peel back the scars
you placed under my chest

I thought we were past this,
this pounding in my chest
this shortness of breath.

This flapping of wings
within my bird box
when your name
appears on my phone screen.

But I suppose
these bones are still shaking,
in need of more time
before they can settle
on their own.

I never wanted skin that heals;
I'd prefer to stay gushing
and watch the world go dark
rather than slowly suffer
as the edges creep together,
leaving behind
patchwork flesh
and hollow bones.

i have done everything
i can
to forget you

and still
i wake to find want
in my hourglass hands

a yearning
for that last drop of sand
to slip through fingers
and finally, land

only then may i be rid
of these time bound shackles
you locked onto my hands

It's starting to happen.

The washing with water
instead of wine;

saying goodnight to darkness
and good morning,
        sunshine.

You don't run through my mind anymore

You sprint.
Leaving behind a trail of dusty memories

Each time
Your stride slightly faster
The dust less dirty

So I wonder:
When will the last time be?
Will it hurt?

Or will it set me free?

I pound my chest
to make sure
my cage remains strong.

It doesn't;
it caves,
cracks
and crumbles

with the thought
of you.

I think that is the difficult part
to wage a war
within yourself;
to breathe in the ash
as the flames burn your throat.
To watch the invaders break down walls
and set ablaze
the library gifted to you
and realize
it may not be
forever and always.

i dread the moment
when i'll forget
what it feels like
to love
you

I scrub the carvings from my bones,
the ones your whispers left behind.

I must be cleansed
before I can be dirtied
by the words
of another lover.

Sometimes
I'll find your name
on my fingers.

Helplessly
scrolling back
through the pixels.

Just to see
if your smile
peels back
the edges of my scabs.

It does.

And, probably,
always will.

You wander through my dreams
With your new lover
As if to tease new memories
With faint smells of the old

Bright red lipstick
Puckered lips stick
Against skin
To which I do not belong

Forced to watch
As roses become nothing
But thorns

It isn't the cut that hurts,
it's the breathing.

The slow bleeding.
The wondering
if sharp shards of your words
can be plucked
from the flesh beneath my skin
to end the suffering.

It was like the first time
I saw you.

My eyes controlled
the beating movement of my chest.
My heart vibrated
across skin
as sweat pooled
in palms.
I began to feel
that tightness in my chest.

Arms began to tingle
as my stomach turned,
unsure if my eyes deceived me.

They didn't.

It was the first time
I saw you

with someone else.

I have to be honest with myself

I find myself in places sleep can't reach
My soul stuck between your fingers
As you harvest my energy
Juicing me for every drop
Leaving behind nothing but an empty effigy

I can't do it anymore
But don't know how to stop
The sapping
The leaking
Without killing the person
You've helped me become

emptiness.

a place once filled
leaving nothing in its stead
but faint scents of memory thread

unable to wash away
the stains on my mind

as I struggle to bind
the pieces of me
you left behind

it's not those moments
where i miss you
that hurt the most
it's the times
when i think of you
halfway through a laugh

Is that you, love?
Knocking away
Like some sort of woodpecker

I wish I could open
And begin to build
Our nest together

But I have yet to repair
My bird box
That you previously
Threw into despair

I am no longer
the hard shell
I once was.

No longer more bone
than embrace.

I am soft,
fleshy.
Easily broken.
Like the beating thing in your chest.

I no longer wonder
where the yellow brick goes.

Your pitter-patter
softens in the distance
as my heartbeat slows.

I can now hear
my heels click
as I step out
onto my own road.

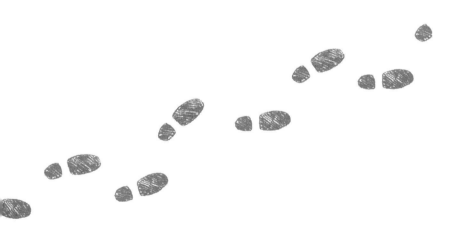

sunlight

----

i do not remember
when i found myself
but do know
it was among the ashes

it was painful.
the shedding of skin
watching the rough,
cracked membrane
fall off my
skeleton

i became witness
to alchemy;
a completely new figure emerged
shimmering
and dancing in sunbeams

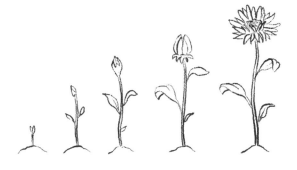

you introduced me to myself

i just wish
we fell in love with him
together

for i now realize
the journey to self-love
doesn't have to be walked alone

just with someone
willing to tend the garden
from which we both have grown

Show me true love
A raw, dirty love

One with bits of dirt caught under fingernails
And calluses on hands
One with soil stuck between teeth
And watered with sweat and tears

Dig deep with me
So our roots grow strong
Plant with me
So our roses grow without thorns

But do not show me love
Born in a shallow pond

I do not wish to drown.

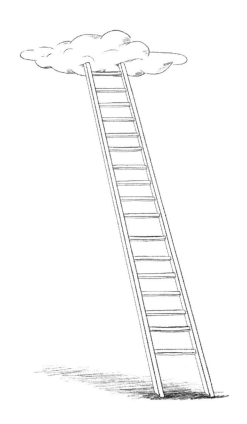

I never understood it before you.

That eruption of shivers
down my spine.
That connectedness to the world,
through you.

You see,
I had become
fearless in feeling.
No longer needing
to keep a goodbye
coiled beneath my tongue.

It allowed us
to rise like giants
and knock our heads
against the sky.

So thank you,
thank you for giving eternity
something to think about.

maybe
you're the book
i always wanted
to write

maybe
just maybe
you're the ghost keeper
i find in my bones

or maybe
just maybe
i had to be broken
by you
to find
myself
in the pieces, left behind

I've kept the phrase
folded behind my tongue.

But can no longer.

I have fallen in love
with myself.

And cannot wait
to unleash the lullaby
found between
my molars.

Keep going.

Fingers emerge blackened by soil
Scratching. Clawing.
Grabbing at earth.

Gasping. Panting.
Breathing in dirt.

Keep going
You tell yourself

You can almost feel the light
Touching your dirty cheeks

Keep going.

The sweet taste of revenge
Fresh on your lips

Keep going!

The fire returning
To your eyes

As you learn:
    You are enough.

you are strongest
when the world
forces you to your knees
shoving earth
into the gaps
between your teeth

and still
you continue
to rise
wearing the soil
as war paint

I feel it in my bones
vibrating in my veins,
sparking at my fingertips.
This fire inside me
igniting my world,
shedding light
on shadowed parts
previously unknown.

I see it now, my full potential.
I just need to reach out and grasp it.
I couldn't before,
but now
but now...
    I no longer fear darkness.

The vibration
of being who you are
is addictive.

You will become
a mountain mover
to scratch the itch
once found.

To make hobby
of resurrection
in your quest
to turn swimmer
into water walker.

Thank you for the pain.
The torment and heartbreak.
The subsequent cloak of self-loathing
and self-doubting.

Thank you for gifting me
the ingredients needed
to prove I am capable of nothing
short of alchemy.

I shimmer, now;
I am the sun
and no longer
fear shadows
cast by the moon.

I will no longer
attempt to cover
the cuts and bruises
gifted to me
during the battles
I swear I have won.

You see,
blemishes need to breathe
so that this patchwork skin
may be threaded together by scars.

For the first time since the war,
I granted my body permission
to rest naked and exposed;
I watched as the bleeding stopped
and wounds began to close.

it was all i could do
to find the space

i didn't have a choice;
i had to
fall apart
to separate myself
from the pain

only now
can i gather the pieces
and rebuild myself
the way i've always wanted
all along

—*Thank You*

i am ready, now
to climb
out of the quicksand of my past
and stand in the present

with enough knowledge
to not let myself sink again

i have decided.

i will no longer
                    cling
        to the words
    or praise
of others

no longer attempt
to photoshop their vision
in hopes that they, too
will see my worth

i have come to realize
that approval only leads to
wasted energy;
energy i now feed my soul
so that i may finally feel
the warmth of my own embrace

Dear self:

I should've loved you sooner.

Tended to your wounds
as if they were my own.
Listened to your words
as you emptied your lungs.

Wrapped you in my arms
without so much space.
Washed away the dirt
the world kicked in your face.

But I am ready now.

And cannot wait
to love my soulmate.

I often found myself
With burning edges,
Smoking as I blew
To suffocate the fire

One day
I held my lungs
And watched the embers
Travel across my skin
And enter into my skeleton

It didn't hurt like I thought it would
It felt good. Powerful. Strong.
The smoldering skin shedding
The purging of poisons

It left me raw and naked
It felt good. Powerful. Strong.
Leaving behind a man with fire in his bones
Leaving me to wonder
  Why didn't I set myself ablaze sooner?

Life is nothing
But peaks and valleys

Transitions between the two
Triggered by some life-changing event
Sometimes good. Usually bad.

Those inflection points
Exist as means to question
"Who am I?"
The answer is often dissatisfied
Sometimes good. Usually bad.

But it's in those moments
Right before the climb
You find yourself
Lost. Questioning. Drowning.
Stripped naked.
Forced to leave bits and pieces behind
Sometimes good. Usually bad.

It has come to my attention
that I am tapped;
completely drained
of you.

No longer able to crank the knob
to spit out words of emotion.
No longer able to fumble through my pockets
to find loose change.

The blood, tears and memories
crystalized in the ink
found on every page.

And so
with a heavy heart
and full lungs
I can finally say:

I no longer have the quarters
to feed this
poetry gumball machine.

i don't think i had met myself
until i was broken,
   really broken.

i remember like it was yesterday
knees bent, kissing the floor
eyes blank, staring at the door
glass broken, nothing to live for

it was only then
could i feel the ache in my bones,
forced to look at the fragmented skeleton
scattered across the tombstone

and ask him

   —How would

                you like

       to be

                  put back

     together?

Love like it's already lost.

It peels back the fear,
leaving behind a raw ball of power
that, some say
can be rolled
forever.

Hurt by the Sun.

It was almost unintentional,
my falling into your light.
It was peaceful.
Beautiful. Calm.

I became mesmerized
by bouncing ringlets
and the warmth from your gaze.

As it would appear,
I soaked up your rays
for a moment too long;
my skin red and raw.
Burned. Charred.

I felt almost helpless,
in my efforts to rid myself of you.
Forced to peel
overcooked pieces of skin
and watch them float away in the wind.

But then slowly,
s l o w l y
I began the healing.
My body releasing your echo
as I regrew my exoskeleton.

No longer lovesick sunburns,
but a stampede of rose petals
sprouting from underneath my skin.

No longer hurt by the sun,
but instead found the light within.

acknowledgments

Thank you to all who have supported me on this journey. I am forever grateful for your love and encouragement.

A special thank you to Eric Koester, Brian Bies, and my editors, Samuel Hawkins II and Jared Rasic, without whom this book would not have been possible.

Lastly, thank you to my family and friends for your advocacy and inspiration. You mean everything to me.